A Surprise for Mrs. O'Malley

Written by Jill Eggleton
Illustrated by Philip Webb

One morning,
Mrs. O'Malley looked
out the window and
there was an alligator
in her backyard.

"**Shivering shudders!**"
said Mrs. O'Malley.
"**Go back to the alley!**"

But the alligator just
stared and glared
and snapped its jaws,
flicked its tail
and sharpened its claws . . .

on Mrs. O'Malley's tree!

Mrs. O'Malley was mad!
She opened the window
and she shouted,

"Can't you hear me?
I don't want you!
Go back to the alley!

Shoo! Shoo!
Shoo!"

But the alligator
wouldn't go.

The next morning,
Mrs. O'Malley looked
out the window and
there were two alligators
in her backyard.

"Shivering shudders!"
said Mrs. O'Malley.
"Go back to the alley!"

But the alligators just
stared and glared
and snapped their jaws,
flicked their tails
and sharpened their claws . . .

on Mrs. O'Malley's fence!

Mrs. O'Malley was mad! She opened the window and she shouted,

"Can't you hear me? I don't want you! Go back to the alley!

Shoo! Shoo! Shoo!"

But the alligators wouldn't go.

The next morning, Mrs. O'Malley looked out the window and there were six alligators in her backyard.

"**Shivering shudders!**" said Mrs. O'Malley. "**Go back to the alley!**"

But the alligators just stared and glared and snapped their jaws, flicked their tails and sharpened their claws . . .

on Mrs. O'Malley's house!

Mrs. O'Malley was mad!
She opened the window
and she shouted,

"Can't you hear me?
I don't want you!
Go back to the alley!

Shoo! Shoo!
Shoo!"

But the alligators
wouldn't go.

The next morning, Mrs. O'Malley looked out the window and there were . . .

alligators, alligators, alligators . . .

all over her backyard!

Mrs. O'Malley was **furious!**

She stamped her feet and she shouted,

"You don't disobey Mrs. O'Malley!

You are going, going, going back to the alley!"

So Mrs. O'Malley phoned the Alligator Man.

The Alligator Man came with his alligator truck. And he took those alligators back to the alley!

"**Good riddance,**" said Mrs. O'Malley.

The next morning,
Mrs. O'Malley went
outside and she saw . . .

eggs,
eggs,
eggs.

Alligator eggs . . .

all over her backyard!

"Shivering, shivering, shudders!"
said Mrs. O'Malley.

The eggs went

And out came alligators.

They stared and glared
and snapped their jaws,
flicked their tails
and sharpened their claws . . .

on Mrs. O'Malley's boots!

"Shivering, shivering,
shudders!"
screeched Mrs. O'Malley.

Guide Notes

Title: A Surprise for Mrs. O'Malley
Stage: Grade 2

Genre: Fiction
Approach: Shared Reading
Processes: Thinking Critically, Exploring Language, Processing Information
Written and Visual Focus: Change of Text Style, Illustrative Text

THINKING CRITICALLY
(sample questions)
- Why do you think the alligators chose to come to Mrs. O'Malley's house?
- Why do you think the alligators wouldn't go back to the alley when Mrs. O'Malley asked them to?
- How do you think the Alligator Man got the alligators into the truck?
- Why do you think the alligators sharpened their claws on things in Mrs. O'Malley's backyard?
- What do you think Mrs. O'Malley will do with all the alligator babies?
- Do you think this story could be true? Why/Why not?

EXPLORING LANGUAGE

Terminology
Title, cover, illustrations, author, illustrator

Vocabulary
Interest words: stared, glared, snapped, flicked, shivering, shudders, good, riddance, furious, disobey, alley, flicked
Contractions: don't, can't, wouldn't
Compound words: backyard
Singular/Plurals: alligator/alligators, claw/claws, man/men
Antonyms: shouted/whispered, morning/night, obey/disobey
Homonyms: too/to/two, tails/tales, there/their, hear/here
Synonyms: mad/angry/furious, shivering/shuddering/shaking, screeched/screamed

Print Conventions
Capital letter for sentence beginnings and names (**Mrs. O'M**alley), periods, exclamation marks, quotation marks, commas, question marks, ellipses, apostrophes